# Rothwell

## in old picture postcards

by
Albert Brown

European Library - Zaltbommel/Netherlands MCMLXXXIII

GB   ISBN 90 288 2337 9

*European Library in Zaltbommel/Netherlands publishes among other things the following series:*

**IN OLD PICTURE POSTCARDS** *is a series of books which sets out to show what a particular place looked like and what life was like in Victorian and Edwardian times. A book about virtually every town in the United Kingdom is to be published in this series. By the end of this year about 75 different volumes will have appeared. 1,250 books have already been published devoted to the Netherlands with the title* **In oude ansichten.** *In Germany, Austria and Switzerland 500, 60 and 15 books have been published as* **In alten Ansichten;** *in France by the name* **En cartes postales anciennes** *and in Belgium as* **En cartes postales anciennes** *and/or* **In oude prentkaarten** *150 respectively 400 volumes have been published.*

*For further particulars about published or forthcoming books, apply to your bookseller or direct to the publisher.*

*This edition has been printed and bound by Grafisch Bedrijf De Steigerpoort in Zaltbommel/Netherlands.*

# INTRODUCTION

Rothwell is an old town. It was first recorded in the Domesday Book, 1087, when it was valued at £8 against a corresponding valuation of £6 for Leeds. Anciently it contained a Royal Hunting Lodge, or Castlet, big enough to accommodate a King of England and his entourage. The Honour, or Barony, of Pontefract, of which Rothwell was part, belonged the Norman family of De Lacy, whose fortune devolved by marriage to the House of Lancaster, of whom the best remembered is John of Gaunt, Duke of Lancaster, who at one time, when his family was young, lived in Rothwell Castle. Legend says he killed the last wild boar in England, at Rothwell, in 1398.

In the eighteenth and nineteenth centuries Rothwell had, at one time, the biggest glass manufactury in Yorkshire, belonging Mr. James Fenton of the colliery family. Mr. Crompton of Woodlesford had a Paper Mill in the goit beside the River Aire. Rothwell Pottery was established in 1767 by two men from South Yorkshire, who leased the glasshouse from Sir William Lowther on a twenty-one years lease. A Match Works that made Lucifer and Firey Jack matches started in 1841, and over the years burnt down half a dozen premises; belonged to Mr. Richard Seanor who lived to see himself proclaimed 'Father of the Match Trade'. In 1854 a gas manufacturing Company was formed to buy out Mr. Young a coal gas pioneer, who had made a gas plant in a stable to supply his neighbours and himself with gaslight.

Coal mining produced its own pioneers. John Blenkinsop, a brilliant engineer, invented and successfully ran a steam locomotive railway hauling coal wagons from Mr. Brandling's coal pits at Middleton to the coal staithes at Leeds fourteen years before George Stevenson invented The Rocket. Blenkinsop is buried in the churchyard at Rothwell. The Fenton family, at Rothwell, were the first coal pit owners to use Fire Engines and pioneer deep coal mining.

On a fairly abundant scale several families were engaged in the manufacturing of Rope and Twine. Other families, on a lesser scale, were in the Basket Making trade. In all forty-six trades are mentioned for Rothwell in the nineteenth century Trades Directories.

From Saxon times Rothwell was an administrative and jurisdictional centre for this district, and had a Manor Court. The function of the Court is self explanatory in its written documentation as seen in this random extraction from the Rolls:

*Manor of Rothwell to wit the Sheriffs Turn View of Frankpledge and Court Leet of our Sovereign Lord the King with the Great Court Baron of Sir William Lowther, Bat. Metcalf Proctor, esq. Henry Elmsall, Clerk, Paul Moore William Wood and William Burnell, Gentlemen, Mary Senior, widow, Richard Houson and the other Lords and Lady's of the Manor of Rothwell aforesaid held there the fourteenth day of October in the twenty first year of the reign of King George the second of Great Brittain and so forth and in the year of our Lord one thousand seven hundred and forty seven.*

The other Lords and Lady's of the Court were neither Lords nor Lady's in the sense of them being of the Peerage, but were mainly of yeoman stock. They tried Copyholders and Freeholders of the Manor of Rothwell for minor offences such as fencing, hedging and ditching, breaking the common pound and for not observing the common rights of the parish, although in earlier times they probably held far greater powers.

The Debtor's Gaol, at Rothwell, was made around the 1660's and stood halfway down the main street until it became redundant, about 1814. It was then transferred to premises on the Marsh, built as a Poorhouse, in 1772. It is presently converted into three dwellings. The only remaining part of the old Debtor's Gaol is the name, Jail Yard.

In writing the texts for this book an effort has been made to mention these heritages as well as things of the not so distant past which people can remember themselves or have been told about by their parents or grandparents. The book has been arranged with the picture postcards, as near as physically possible, in walking order.

Apart from farming the principle trade of the district has always been coal mining, but that has greatly declined over the last fifty years. Within the next two years the last of the pits in Rothwell will have closed.

1. The clue to this picture is on the board behind the steer. In 1897, Queen Victoria had been on the throne sixty years. Ten years earlier Rothwell had celebrated her Golden Jubilee in great style. Rothwell now wanted to do even better. There had been no bullock roasting at Rothwell since the end of the Crimean War; so it was planned to repeat that for the Diamond Jubilee. Mr. Stephen Wilkinson, a noted local butcher, was appointed to select a suitable beast at Wakefield Cattle Market. This is that beast with Stephen, age sixty-seven, at the head, Thomas at the tail and his brother, John, behind.

2. Early stages in the decoration of Rothwell for the Diamond Jubilee of Queen Victoria. The commonly called Bread Arch is mis-leading. It was not made of bread. It was supposed to be a Gothic Arch inspired by the Gates of York. Food, left over from the public tea, was shared out here between the aged and the pauper poor; from which the name probably arose. Where the house stands next the arch was once the entrance to a shoeing forge belonging Sam Atkinson, blacksmith, who lived in the corner shop. The early pillar gas lamp outside T. Shearman's did not use a mantle, but depended on a naked flame for illumination.

3. Ineson's are recorded at Rothwell since 1784, but Charles Ineson and his wife were born at Birstall. They came to Rothwell in 1876 where he set himself up as a Printer and Draper. In 1880, when Andrew Marshall, Postmaster at Rothwell since 1872, announced his retirement the Post Office was removed to the premises of Mr. Ineson, the new Postmaster. Posed for the Celebrations this shows Charles Ineson and wife, right; son, Luke, wife and children, bedroom window; son, James, and wife and Mr. and Mrs. Newsome. In those days the Post Office was open six full days and until noon on Sunday.

4. Celebrations! This block of buildings, first seen on an eighteenth century map, lay east of Rothwell Vicarage; with gardens extending into the Marsh and alongside the Vicarage gardens. The whole complex also included the Fleece Beer House, a timber structure of venerable age. The first known owners of this property was the Hindle family at the end of the eighteenth century. When a Miss Hindle put up the estate for sale in 1892, it was bought by Charles Ward. He sold the Fleece plot to the Rothwell Local Board as land on which to build the new Council Offices. The spire behind belongs to the Church Schools.

5. This, shop-in-a-corner, was Jack Brown's, sweets tobacconist and fancy goods at the end of the 1914-1918 War. At the time of this photo it looks more like a general store. Was the celebration for King Edward and Queen Alexandra, in 1902; or for King George and Queen Mary, in 1911? At one time it belonged to John Brown, cabinet maker, then to Maria Brown, druggist, and it is on record that her deceased husband was buried at Rothwell in an iron bound coffin eleven feet deep. A member of Rothwell Grave Club: his grave was watched over for five nights as a precaution against grave robbers.

6. The cottage where Ma Bond lived and sold cigarettes and mineral waters, sixty years ago. In the seventeenth century this was Witch Country. Catherine Earl, the Rothwell Witch, lived not far away. Descendants of her brother may have lived in this cottage. More sinister, however, was the reputation of Dungeon Lane that joins this road opposite the end tree on the picture, right. The name is probably a corruption of Dung-houses, a reputed asylum for lunatics and other deranged folk; who, at times of the full moon, often went beserk and brought terror into the lives of the local community.

7. This picture, date circa 1910, reflects the rural nature of upper Royds Lane then. A copse of tall trees with branches showing, top right, lasted up to the 1914-1918 War. The road, anciently, was part of the Kings Highway between Leeds and Pontefract in the days before the making of Turnpike roads. The Lane at this point, known as Waterloo Corner, turns dogleg towards Rothwell village. Once it continued straight on almost to the precincts of Oulton Hall, from where it swung westwards, by Beeston Wood, to connect up with Oulton Lane near the gates of Rothwell Park.

8. Waterloo Corner is the official name, but to 'Rodillers' it was Keepers Corner. Entrance to the Keepers Cottage is behind the public seat. This is the view looking north, the last looks south. Oulton Hall estate was strictly preserved with a Head Keeper and assistants until after the 1914-1918 War. In springtime the fields were dotted with tiny hatching pens. Each one held a domestic hen sitting on a clutch of pheasant or partridge eggs. In those days game birds, rabbits and 'mad march hares' could be seen in the fields or wandering in Royds Lane, at any time.

9. Public seats were provided by Rothwell Local Board as early as 1884. These children are outside the gate to the Cricket Field, acquired by Rothwell Cricket Club in 1875. During matches, if a cricket ball was hit out of the ground across the lane and into the next field, it was a standing agreement that any boy who found it, and returned the ball, would get sixpence. Behind the seat is the Dodgecroft. It was once an *open field*. Evidence of this mediaeval economy remained until the 1920's when it was ploughed and made into allotments. On the other side of the lane is the field of 'the beast with two tails'.

10. Richard Fox junior started in the haulage business the hard way, on foot. He began by hawking baskets of produce bought in Leeds Market, from door to door round Rothwell. He bought a pony and cart to extend the business and branched out into light haulage. Then into passenger carrying with cabs and a wagonette. He saw a future in motorised transport and purchased this, solid rubber tyre, char-a-banc. It could go faster and further than a horse-drawn vehicle. It had the comfort of better seats and a hood that could be raised in bad weather. It also had problems. It soon over-heated and frequent stops had to be made to cool the engine.

11. In the history of Rothwell this is a new thoroughfare. In early times, the Marsh was a parcel of waste land. Its wet nature, rough herbage and lack of soil made it useless except as common adjustment for geese. It lay between the properties south of Rothwell Street and the Saint Clements lands of the Duchy of Lancaster. Taken about 1908 this shows (in the distance) the entrance to the spring on the roadside, behind the hedge, right; from which the street gets its name. Barraclough's (bracket gaslamp on the farmhouse end) was a rhubarb farm. The two low sheds are forcing houses for the rhubarb.

12. Taken before the 1914-1918 War, it shows the Wesleyan Methodist Chapel's Annual Whitsuntide Procession through the streets. Those in the second half of the walk are passing the 'rival' Primitive Methodist Chapel which obscures the Council Offices. The stone row of cottages and Holmes Square, behind them, is now Marsh Street Car Park. Behind the iron railings is Marsh Villa, the first, licensed, Rothwell Working Mens Club. In the foreground is the wall of the Pinfold, or town pound. In the distance, 'Bedpost' Terrace, and behind, the half timbered black and white premises at the foot of Swithens Street.

13. The administrative body at Rothwell, from the time of the Vestry to the Local Board in 1873, all made use of the Church Sunday School premises, built in 1814, as a meeting place. With the proposed extension of the Board to an Urban District Council it was decided, in 1892, to build a more suitable building to accommodate a full time staff and a comfortable room for the elected members of the Council. A site on the Marsh, occupied by the Fleece Beer House and gardens, was bought from Mr. Chas. Ward, grocer. The foundation stone was laid in 1895 and the Council Offices opened 8th of June, 1896.

14. In the early days of Methodism, at Rothwell, services were held in a stable in Butcher Lane, belonging to Mr. North, a well to do farmer. After his death the property and land were conveyed to thirteen trustees of the Methodist faith by John North's widow and eldest son, for five shillings. John Wesley preached in this chapel on Sunday, August 9th, 1772, also from the steps of the Cross and once in Gaol Fold. The later chapel, opened in 1880, was enlarged and altered over the years. It was demolished about ten years ago and the present building, erected as a Sunday School in 1900, was converted into the chapel.

15. An old cliché says 'all chapels are much of a muchness', but not all chapels can boast a personal link with John Wesley. The deeds of this Wesleyan chapel, dated 1764, names John and Charles Wesley along with eight local persons as co-Trustees of 'all that newly erected house, or tenement, with stable and yard (to the use of) — John Wesley, late of Lincoln College, Oxford, Clerk, and such other persons as he shall nominate to preach and expound God's Holy Word'. He also preached in the chapel of the converted stable, and the board made for him to stand on at his out-door meetings is still retained.

16. Lion House was never a great work of art. This photograph, taken during the general demolition of the area, shows that forelorn look of all abandoned property. The most prominent aspect of the house was the stone lion on the parapet. The story connected with it, told to many generations of children, goes like this: 'When the lion hears the church clock strike twelve, midnight, it gets up from its perch and goes down to the beck for a drink', or as some would say, 'down to the Sterroid Well, for a drink'. Which ever way it is told the operative quote is *'When the lion hears the clock'* — or the whole thing becomes a nonsense.

17. This is one of the most ancient landmarks of Rothwell. Batty in his 'History of Rothwell' dates the granting of a Charter for a market at Rothwell as early as 1250 A.D. There is no evidence to support this. Palmer's Index No 99, compiled in 1889, the official list of Charters of Markets and Fairs, only lists one Charter for Rothwell. It is dated 6th February, ninth Henry 4th, or 1408. Like Batty it reads, granted to Rothwell within our Honour of Pontefract, 'a certain markett within our town every week upon Wednesday forever to be holden'.

18. This was the mediaeval heart of Rothwell. Nearby stood the Maypole and the stocks. On market days stalls were erected along the whole length of Rothwell Street. On the site of Lion House would be the Market Reeves cottage, where from an elevated position, perhaps a bedroom window, he could watch all that went on in the market. This could not start until he rang the Starting-bell. All transactions ended when he rang the market Closing-bell. That was the Law. Where three ladies stand by the shop, was Nanny Stead's Dame School; and in a room above, a branch of the I.L.P. was formed, in 1893.

19. These premises probably belonged to a family who were maltsters as the buildings included a stable, drying kiln, malt kiln, granary and chambers. In 1840 it belonged Elizabeth Hindle, relict of John. She was then living in the west wing. In the centre premises, lived John Lewis, grocer, who had the outbuildings, and the east wing had become two cottages. After Mrs. Hindle's death her house was occupied in succession by Wm Handforth, a coal miner, and his son-in-law David Brears, Journeyman shoemaker; followed by Charles Hampson, Boot and Shoemaker. Then as shown by Harry Edwards, greengrocer.

20. Continuing the history of these premises, London House; Mr. Lewis was followed by Samuel Batty, Tailor and Draper, whose son John Batty, author of the *History of Rothwell*, was thirteen years of age in 1851. Robert Holliday, grocer, and his daughter, Mary, a deaf and dumb dressmaker, were the next tenants. They were followed by Charles Ward, from Carlton, whose family retained a grocery business here until the premises were demolished. Thomas Stephenson, a Tea Dealer, living down the street in 1841, had by 1851 moved into the cottage next to the Holliday's and recorded as Druggist and Registrar.

21. Looking at this dilapidated structure it is hard to imagine it as the west wing of the finest house in Rothwell — two hundred years ago. The east wing still stands much altered in the guise of a modern shop. Mr. Holmes, a nineteenth century property developer, built over the Elizabethan paved court yard (where a cavelier is said to lie buried) and brought the buildings into line with the road. The middle shop in this photo was Arthur Sunderland's, barber. He sold cricket equipment, played for the Tradesmen's Cricket Club and talked barber-talk about his hero, Herbert Sutcliffe, Yorkshire and England opening batsman.

22. Rothwell, 1905, plus the 'new fangled' tramway. Levelling the road for the trams meant people living in the old cottage, left, had to go down steps into the groundfloor rooms. The modern premises next door stand on the site of the Debtors Gaol. Mr. Dickinson, who owned the property, is named twice on this photo. The pork butcher shop, with the awning, belonged Mr. Keitel; and in between see the plaque on the wall, The Midland Bank. On the right, in deep shadow, is Holmes and Batty, Drapers. The next door barber shop housed Rothwell's first public telephone. The block was six premises back-to-back.

23. This later photo of the Post Office, now one shop, shows Chas. Ineson with son, James, who continued the drapery business in these premises until 1947. The Post Office was transferred to new premises across the road in 1916. The postman was handily placed, he lived next door to the Post Office. Two doors away, later Bridge's, bakers, were the first premises of the Leeds Co-op Society, at Rothwell. The ginnel was once a street leading into the Marsh. The shop beyond was Joe Stead's, sweets and tobacconist; he wore a velvet jacket and Mandarin hat when serving in the shop.

24. Rothwell Model Brass Band had its headquarters at the Coach and Horses. In 1872 Mr. Joseph Charlesworth, of the Colliery owning family, gave a free-hold plot of land and lent the money 'to build the finest Bandroom in Yorkshire'. On Saturday nights members and non-members could get together to listen to the band. For the sum of two pence (bring your own mug) you could sit, listen and sup free beer until the barrel was empty. After the band split into two factions, in 1881, these five were members of 'The old Band', the drinkers, who had retained possession of the Bandroom.

25. Showing the street still lit by gas lamps in 1930. The tram track is still there and Percy Kempshall, newsagent, had moved into the 'Bee Hive'. The three houses next Jail Yard are there; only just. See the iron plate holding the wall in. Next, now Mil-ric, and two other cottages date from Jacobean times. Further along the street, Sam Heaton's butcher shop and neighbours, now replaced by Arthur Carr and the Gas Showroom. On the other side of the road the space between London House, in shadow; and the gable end of Mr. Bushe's fruit shop, in sunshine, is the National School yard.

26. Bottom of Hargreaves Street outside Matt. Ward's shop. The flat horse drawn cart carrying the Sunday School organ and attendant musicians, which always led the chapel procession. An annual event held on a Sunday close to Whitsuntide. The procession halted at pre-determined places to sing hymns. This assembly is one stop on from the procession shown in photo No. 12. On Whit-Monday afternoon there was a paper-bag tea, childrens sports and adults tug-of-war or single wicket bowling, etc. in the cricket field, if the weather was good. Otherwise they were held in the Sunday Schools.

27. Tramcar passing Black Bull Hotel (standing back, right). It replaced Tom Hardacre's Bull, licensed premises; early nineteenth century. If the Cross was the old forum of Rothwell, this area around the lamp was the new forum. During the first years of this century non-working colliers met here to discuss world affairs: such as pigeon racing and cricket. It was the new age of speed. Trams, motor cars and steam wagons came racing through Rothwell at speeds of up to eighteen miles per hour. A good job that providence had provided the Coach and Horses and the Black Bull where shattered nerves could be provided for!!!

28. Depicting the Victorian and Edwardian fervour for young peoples processions. This is thought to be a Rechabite Demonstration. The Temperance Society, a movement for total abstinence from alcoholic drink, was strong at Rothwell, at the end of the century. The Church had its own Temperance Mission and a Band of Hope, as has the chapels, but the Rechabites and The Little White Ribboners, at Rothwell, appear to have been sponsored soley by the Temperance Society.

29. A typical scene on Remembrance Sunday. This was the Dedication of Rothwell War Memorial, November, 1923. The corner site was formerly part of Whitehall Farm, at the commencement of Oulton Lane. It had been a farm yard with a stable, cow mistals and a barn with straw littered yard. Behind the soldier is Whitehall Garth, but more commonly called The Flower Show Field because it was here Rothwell Flower and Horticultural Society held their annual Flower Show and Gala.

30. Richard Fox junior, before the making of Meynell Avenue into Commercial Street, built the house and premises, near the beck, in 1899. It was stated at the Local Board enquiry that permission was needed from Mr. Fox before work could start on the bridge, because he owned a strip of land 8' wide and 8' long where the buttresses of the bridge would have to go. He was a contractor to football teams, etc. carrying them to away fixtures. He ran horse cabs for weddings and funerals. A service still supplied by his son, now with Rolls Royce limousines.

31. Rothwell from the top of the tower of Holy Trinity Church. Taken about 1922, it shows the newly built Picture House. The smaller white building behind was built in 1838 as the Ebonezer Chapel. When a larger chapel was made in Marsh Street, in 1884, the Ebenezer became a storage place for Mr. Seanor's Match Works. In 1922 it was a manufactury for Mazonium, a grate varnish for iron, coal fired, ranges. The street, left, is Ingram Parade. The street, right, from its junction with Commercial Street in front of the Hare and Hounds Inn, down over the beck and swinging round in front of the church, is Church Street.

32. In 1776, Mary Chapman, an unmarried mother, gave birth to a son William. The scandal forced her to leave Oulton and apply for support, for herself and her son, from the Overseers who lodged her in a pauper cottage near Rothwell Church. When the time came they apprenticed young William to a bricklayer. His descendants remained in the bricklaying and building trade into the twentieth century. They built many notable buildings including the Mechanics Institute, the Board Schools, in Carlton Lane, and the Council Offices. This is a later William Chapman, his son Howath, and their wives.

33. No church at Rothwell is shown in the Domesday Book, but a church at Rothwell was given as an endowment to the Priory of Saint Oswald, by Robert de Pontefract, in 1123. This one is probably the third church on this site. The marauding Scots army, it is said, burnt down the church in 1318. Some stones in the fabric show signs of burning. Evidence of an early church is seen in two ancient sculptured stones of Saxon origin, and a portion of double-billet moulding that is characteristicly Norman. In the cottage, right, lived Levi Barker, who made clogs for pit men at 2/6d. a pair.

34. The interior of the Church of the Holy Trinity has been much altered in the last two hundred years. Gone is the ancient stained glass to be replaced with windows of modern coloured glass. On the other hand the plastered-over roof of Commonwealth times was re-discovered during extensive alterations in 1841, to show a beautiful bossed oak roof, now fully restored, painted and gilded. Introduced in 1858, the bench pews have solid oak ends with finials carved with foliage, figures of birds and beasts. Preserved in a glass case in the vestry is a unique and venerable garment known traditionally as *John of Gaunts coat*.

35. One of the reasons for assuming the history of Rothwell goes back to Saxon times, is the name of the mill race, the Goit, a Saxon word. Also that, in King Edward the Confessor's time, a corn mill at Rothwell is recorded as worth two shillings per annum. In this photo the mill is the building behind the mill mens cottages (foreground). The whole is built on an island formed by the mill dam, behind; the mill goit on the north and the overflow water from the dam, to the south, which came together here. This was the ford crossing from Wood Lane to the bottom of Cross Hill, into Rothwell town.

36. At this point the waters of two streams merge to form the pond to provide the water to work the corn mill. The three men on the raft are, in the 'boater' with the punting pole, Tom Barrett, miller, and middle of three generations of Tom Barrett's at Rothwell corn mill, in the centre is Basil Abbishaw and Tom Brook, seated, one time police constable. Just visible behind is the column of grout, the only remaining evidence of Rothwell Castle, former Hunting Lodge and 'Hospitium' of King John.

37. Rothwell Manor House, across Wood Lane from the church, was once a much larger complexity of buildings. To wit a mediaeval Royal Castlet 'beloved' of King John. Here, John of Gaunt built a bridge of stone from the castle to the church. The same building was in a ruinous state in 1486 when King Henry VII gave the Manor Garth to his 'trusty and wel-beloved Roger Hopton, Esquire, Gent, Husher of our Chamber' to build himself a house. The timber frame of that house, erected in 1487, was taken from the ruins when it was demolished in 1976. It had been lived in continuously for almost five hundred years.

38. It could be said the railway station at Rothwell was tangible evidence for a great conception that went wrong. A railway that aged, withered and became incontinent before it was born. In 1838 a railway gratis and pre-funded was offered to Rothwell and refused. The enormity of this folly festered for forty years before steps were taken to rectify that mistake. The most formidable opposition to the new project then came from the very railway company Rothwell had rejected in 1838. The East and West Union Junction (Rothwell) Railway Company had planned to carry freight direct to Hull and London.

39. The Rothwell Company (E. & W.U.J. Railway) had planned to start with an initial twenty-five miles of track, Rothwell to Drax, in 1880. This would have provided them with a connection to the main line from Edinburgh to London. This shrunk to about six miles of track all within the parish of Rothwell. A start was made in March 1880. Work progressed steadily with pack and shovel until it was possible to bring in two steam excavators of American design known as 'American Devils'. Each one capable of doing the work of fifty men. The first freight trains of the Rothwell railway were running into Rothwell Station by July 1891.

40. This photo of a little boy on the pastures with the Rose Pit in the background has a very rural look. The pit sunk in 1850. Batty says, was so named because of the profusion of wild roses growing in the vicinity. During the sinking of the shaft workmen cut through an underground stream thought to be the source of both the Church Well, in Wood Lane, and the Sterroid Well, on the Pastures. Shortly afterwards the Church Well ran dry, but the Sterroid Well was unaffected. They stopped winding coal at the Rose Pit in the 1920's, but kept it as a winding shaft for men and supplies.

41. Second photo of Rose Pit, about twenty years later, depicting a more industrial aspect, and yet there seems to be very little, if any, difference in the buildings (the mill dam in the foreground is still providing the power for the corn mill). What does show clearly is the growth in size of the waste tip that continued to grow until long after the winding of coal had ceased. It was always a shaft with water problems despite the reputed spending of three quarters of a million pounds to cure the fault. The stopping of the Church Well, it seems, was an expensive mistake all round.

42. Mr. Goodchild, author of *The Coal Kings of Yorkshire,* says the Fanny pit was sunk in 1867, which is only half a truth. A pit was sunk by J. & J. Charlesworth beside the North Midland Railway, off Bullock Lane and near to the Aire and Calder Canal, in that year. Printed evidence calls it The Midland Pit. Locally it was known as Bullock Lane Pit. It was in 1911 that the new Fanny shaft was sunk, since when it has been called Fanny Pit. In 1922 a new sinking pit was made to improve the underground ventilation. It was an upcast shaft. The old Midland shaft remained as a ventilation shaft until after the sinking shaft was completed.

43. The Liberal Club in Wood Lane was two buildings in one. The north end was built at the end of the 1800's by the Rothwell Railway Company as the Station Masters House. The builders, at the time, diverted a path to square the grounds of the new house, but the R.U.D.C. made the company pull down and re-build it to leave the right of way to the Padfoot Steps in its original form. When the house became vacant in 1919, the Rothwell Liberal Club bought the property and extended the south end of the house. The idea of a big club with big membership did not materialise and the debts incurred eventually bankrupted them.

44. The Liberal Association at Rothwell first hired two rooms in a house near the Cross, in 1881, to make a club. It consisted of a reading room and a room for political meetings and discussion. This club folded when Rothwell I.L.P. poached the more radical elements of the Whig Party into its own ranks. A new attempt by the Liberals to form a Liberal Club, at Rothwell, was made in 1888 at a meeting called in Mr. Ely's Temperance Hotel. This photo was taken in an even later Liberal Club, the ex-Local Board-cum-Church Sunday School premises in Churchfields, about 1910.

45. The downhill road into Rothwell has always had its problems. As long ago as the fourteenth century, Dr. Johnson records Wood Lane as 'the great cut way'. In the sixteenth century travellers across *The Haigh,* from the gate of Rothwell made their way as best they could for there was no road. The present road was first made under the *Enclosure of Rothwell Haigh Act, in 1783.* The coming of the electric tramway, in 1904, made necessary the levelling and regulating of the contours of Wood Lane. In the middle of the hill the high ground had to be cut back by a yard or more, as shown in the photograph.

46. If you think little has changed on this part of Wood Lane note the footpath, left, and the old lady looking out of the Misses Elstob's Drug store. This path is only half paved with flagstones. On the other side of the road the footpath is all dirt. There is no Baptist Chapel, only a grass close. One arm of the fingerpost points down Haigh Road, '24 miles to York'. The other fingers point to Rothwell or Leeds. That is a lockup butcher shop at the bottom of Spibey Lane; known as Windmill Road until the windmill was removed. See the gas lamp, and the open-end tram that in winter was open to wind, hail and snow.

47. The Workhouse was built in 1900 and partly occupied in 1902. It included Darby and Joan Cottages, Vagrants Departments, Male and Female. A work house and infectious diseases buildings. Also stables for horses, styes for pigkeeping and a pump house for Sea Therapy, with a Master and Matron in charge. Rothwell first built a Poorhouse in 1772. After many changes Rothwell, under the Local Board, joined in Union with Hunslet. This Workhouse on Rothwell Haigh was erected to serve that Union. It is now St. Georges Hospital.

48. The Hopton family for many years had a market garden in Low Shops Lane. The lane has a history of its own. It was made under the Enclosure Act of 1783. On the map of the Act it is shown as 'Lord Stourton Coal Road' (a fine title for an un-made dirt road), from Mr. Fenton's coal pits to the road leading from the Leeds to Wakefield Turnpike Road, into Rothwell town. From the back of this card we learn the old lady was about eighty years of age in 1900. Morley Hopton, her grandson, is remembered with his son, as being farriers, at premises off Marsh Street, known as Blacksmiths Yard.

49. Taken about 1909, it shows a group of fitters by the beam of the 'New Engine', at J. & J. Charlesworth's Low Shops. When this firm took over Fenton's Rothwell Haigh Colliery, in 1820, they concentrated the whole drainage pumping system of the Rothwell Haigh pits, serving twenty shafts or more, at Low Shops. The old water weighted drawing machinery and two steam pumping engines, The Green and The Piccadilly, were replaced by two Boulton and Watt machines, known as the Old Engine and the New Engine. Installed in 1820, this latter engine continued in work until 1929.

50. A 1902 photo showing, from the right, Head Carpenter and Wheelright, William Hartley, who worked at Low Shops until turned eighty years of age. Next to him his grandson, Hartley Banks, and Joseph Chadwick, nephew. They were responsible for all woodwork at Low Shops, and with resident joiners, at all other J. & J. Charlesworth pits in the area. They repaired horse ambulances, block carts and wooden pit tubs. They maintained colliery offices, engine houses, pit headgear and underground ventilation doors. In short anything made of wood, including coffins for the victims of pit accidents.

51. It is hard to realise in these days of automated and semi-automated coal mining, that only about half a lifetime ago there was next to no mechanical coal getting, or mechanical haulage of coals in the pits. As late as 1920 all the local pits used ponies for underground haulage. On the surface instead of heavy lorries and mechanised shovels etc., the work was done by shire horses. This was the reason and the need for a well manned shoeing forge and farriers shop. In 1924 there were twenty-four shire horses stabled at Beeston Pit. One hundred and sixty ponies were stabled underground at Fanny Pit, in 1922, but less than twenty ten years later.

52. J. & J. C. loco on the line between Low Shops and Beeston Pit, behind the Workhouse. There was a tramway here long before steam locomotives were invented. The Fenton's used bullocks to pull coal wagons along this road from pits west of the Turnpike road, to the top of the hill, and down an incline tramway to the coal staithes on the River Aire. That wagon way made a level crossing of Jaw Bones Lane, now Wood Lane. When steam loco's came into use a bridge was made and the trains passed under the road. A new engine in 1880 got stuck in the bridge and a new and higher bridge had to be made.

53. Anciently this area was part of the Royal Hunting Park of Rothwell Hay. It was exclusively preserved and common travellers had to go round it. Only people about the Kings business, or the Kings tenants with Common Rights within the park, had right of entry. A long departure from those days to the lighting of public roads with gas lamps. There was a hollow brass tube at the end of the lamplighters stick to hold a lighted candle with which the lamps were lit by pushing the stick into the lamp from the underneath. Lamps were only lit three weeks in four. On the week of the full moon no lamps were lighted.

Jaw Bones, Rothwell Haigh.

54. Batty says the Fenton family brought the whale jaw bones from America and used them as gate posts to their house in Woodhouse Hill. They were removed from that position when the house was sold and later re-erected as gate posts to a close on the corner of Wood Lane and the Turnpike Road. In 1904 this land was bought by the Electric Tramway Company for the building of Tram Sheds and other Works. The Jaw Bones were then taken down and re-erected over the footpath to be used as a lamp standard. The present Jaw Bones, now on the other side of the road, date from 1967.

55. Leeds to Wakefield Road, at Lofthouse. Once a hamlet in the old parish of Rothwell. The Rose and Crown Hotel is the only part of this group remaining. On the left, the house beyond the lamp post is Pyemont House. Three hundred years ago the Pyemont family were one of the leading yeoman families of Lofthouse. They were coal miners, farmers and merchants. Surviving documents show they supplied General Wade's army which camped overnight at Lofthouse, with horse fodder, after the Jacobite rising in Scotland. Note the horse collar and harness outside the cottage, on right of picture.

56. Taken at Lofthouse near the present Grammar School. These workmen are assembled outside the local Highways Depot of the Rothwell U.D.C. The previous authority, The Rothwell Local Board, tried many ways of maintaining the roads. From direct labour by Council employees to letting 'the roads to private contractors'. In 1874 the hours of work fixed for road men, were, in Summer, 6 a.m. to 5 p.m., Monday to Friday, and 6 a.m. to 2 p.m. Saturday. Hours of work in winter were from dark to dark, or until 2 p.m. Saturday. Under the R.U.D.C. the workday was shortened by one hour. Starting time being 7 a.m. other details the same.

57. No. 25 one of the early double decker open topped electric trams. A glorious way to travel on a hot summers afternoon, but an awful experience in winter, blizzard conditions. The tram lines to Leeds (Thwaite Gate) and Wakefield were laid down by, or for, the Wakefield based West Riding Electric Tramway Company, who ran trams between Wakefield and Leeds; but only Leeds trams ran to Rothwell. This was all part of a complicated fares system agreed between the two companies which meant that through passengers on the Rothwell route had to pay twice on every journey.

58. What was the attraction of the pit officials' houses at the top of Bell Hill? Evidently photography was still so new that the sight of a man setting up his camera was enough to bring everyone outside to get into the picture. On the other side of the pit gates to where the little boy sits over the letter box in the wall, there was a Pinfold in the days when this was a Turnpike road. Batty says there used to be a public house here, called The Blue Ball, and lower down the hill, during the making of the cutting, in 1823, a Roman coffin of Millstone grit was uncovered containing the body of a young girl.

59. Rear of Beeston pit houses it shows Mr. Harold Kempshall, his wife and friends. Note how closely the motor car resembles a horse vehicle. The coachwork almost matches that of a pony trap or wagonette. The wood spoke wheels and the chassis on eliptical springs are much the same as a horse cab. The first motor cars were mechanical horses with steering wheels instead of reins. Newly innovated are the pneumatic tyres and they have no tread! The headlamps are acetylene carbide gas lamps. There is no windscreen or hood so there was a real need for good waterproof clothes and goggles.

60. No. 9 another loco based at Low Shops, with driver Basil Abbishaw and mates. They operated between the East and West, Rothwell railway line at Robin Hood, Beeston Pit, Victoria Pit, and down the Old Run to Charlesworth's Land Sales Depot at Stourton. In 1870 the Beeston Pit was sunk to get the Beeston Bed coal. It was then the largest pit in the district. In 1874 a report on the pit shows the ventilation system was based on a pit bottom furnace. If the furnace man was diligent and kept a brisk fire burning the volume of air passing into the workings was enough for the miners needs.

Cycle Series, No. 2.—Leeds to Methley.    "John o' Gaunts"

61. John O' Gaunt's Hotel on Pontefract Road and not a garage or petrol filling station in sight! There is a four wheel covered van and a block cart, horse drawn, of course. That is the reason for the open shed alongside the hotel, whose slogan was, *Good accommodation for man and beast*. A sign over the door proclaimes 'Here stayed John of Gaunt one time Duke of Lancaster' (not strictly true). The Barnsdale Turnpike Road was made in 1822, and the hotel shortly afterwards. A tavern is mentioned at Rothwell Haigh in 1398, when John of Gaunt organised a party to hunt wild boar there.

62. An early mechanical horse that ate coal and belched steam. One hundred years ago several firms in Hunslet built this type of steam traction monster and tested them on the roads of Rothwell. Hitched behind the engine is a wagon, and possibly a second or third wagon. Heavy road trains with wagons carrying an average of twelve tons of building stone each, caused great damage to local roads made for horse drawn traffic. The only consolation for the authorities was that it was illegal to work steam engines on the road after sunset. The writing over the door reads, *Kind friends prefer, once far-famed Duke of Lancaster.*

63. It is hard to envisage a more isolated place for a Smallpox Hospital. Today it is easily over-looked in a solid block of modern housing. A widespread outbreak of Smallpox in the winter of 1887-88, alerted Rothwell Local Board to a need for hospital accommodation. The engine shed of the Board's steam road engine was estimated to be big enough to accommodate nursing staff and three beds for patients. February 4th, 1888, it was announced, as a precautionary measure, the Local Board had rented a cottage in Styebank Lane. The first patient was Emma Arnett, a child from Oulton, admitted 20th April 1888.

64. Look how smart they are dressed in their Sunday best! This was taken at the foot of Sandy (Styebank) lane in 1911. It was then a lonely and remote area. Eight years later it was my job to walk this lane every day to fetch milk from Mr. Craven's farm in a milk churn on hand propelled wheels. A little way beyond this point the hill becomes steeper, passing between grassy banks on which grew tall trees whose overhanging branches formed a leafy archway over the road. The only building in this vicinity, in 1888, was the cottage, rented at 3/6d. a week, as the Smallpox Isolation Hospital.

65. This scene in Springhead Park was taken on Infirmary Sunday, when local brass bands would play selections of music and take a collection on behalf of the Leeds Infirmary. Not to be mistaken with Infirmary Demonstration Day. In the foreground, partly obscured by the contour of the land, is part of the great carriage driveway through the park from the main gaites in Oulton Lane. In those days Springhead Park was only a small part of what is now Rothwell Park. The rest of the park was then sub-divided into fields, by hedge rows, as shown in the photograph.

66. When Rothwell U.D.C. bought the land to make Rothwell Park the deal included Springhead House. When this picture was taken the house and estate belonged to Mr. and Mrs. Atkinson and it was by their leave that it became the site for the Annual Infirmary Demonstration. In 1895 the Cadets of H.M.S. 'Indefatigable' came to Rothwell to demonstrate physical training exercises and other disciplines. The show concluded with 'The Storming of Port Arthur' including musketry fire, cannonade and fireworks effects. The mock-up ship H.M.S. 'Springhead' being placed on the beck as part of the backcloth to the display.

67. The Rothwell Temperance Band was formed out of the Rothwell Model Brass Band, in 1881, after a disagreement on policy concerning drink. Here they are shown wearing their first band uniforms, which were in fact, second-hand Lancers Uniforms. It is said they looked very smart and soldiery; until they were seen by a serving officer who warned them they were breaking the law by wearing them. In 1909 the fee for twenty-two men playing three days at the Infirmary Gala, amounted to £6-12-0. Always a contesting band, the Temperance, in 1927, won first prize at Belle Vue, and then won the Grand Shield, at Crystal Palace.

68. A close up of H.M.S. 'Springhead' on the beck, in 1895. The Cadets, then, proved to be such a successful attraction they were invited back to perform in the Jubilee year, three days Gala and Infirmary Day Celebrations. This time they gave 'Episodes of a Soldiers Life' supported by fireworks, musketry fire and — the cry of the wounded, when it was discovered that one of the Cadets had received a ball in the arm. A doctor in the crowd was quickly in attendance. He removed the ball, bandaged the arm and put it in a sling. At the end of the day the lad, apparently, was little the worse for his experience.

69. Posing for this picture, Rothwell Angling Club. The same group taken from a longer range shows the Bowling Green Hotel in the background, perhaps the clubs headquarters. The man in the shirt sleeves could be Ben Taylor, the landlord. This public house was built towards the end of the nineteenth century. At that time the way to it was up Taylor Lane. Later a more direct way was made from the hotel into Oulton Lane and nearer to the village. As the name suggests it was made equipped with two bowling greens. Later for some obscure reason the name was changed to Rabbit Trap Hotel.

70. Oulton was from ancient times a part of Rothwell parish. In 1827 Mr. John Blaydes, esq., of Leeds and Oulton bequeathed the funds necessary for building and endowing the Church of St. John; in the Early English Pointed Style. Not far away a Quaker Burial Ground sold to the sect by Sarah Metcalf, of Oulton, was recently lost under a programme of landscaping. In 1879 Mr. Metcalf, sexton, was working in St. John's churchyard when he was accosted by a tramp person named D'Arcy who tried to sell him a watch. Mr. Metcalf declined the offer and D'Arcy killed him, in daylight, and in front of witnesses.

71. This fine old house is older than the date shown on the beam. Edward Tailor married a child bride, Isabel Lumly, of Rothwell. Tradition says the Tailor's and Lumly's lived side by side in Rothwell Town until Edward restored the old house, at Oulton, in 1611. This may very well be true because a fireplace in the house is dated a century earlier. A report by Leeds University gives the information, 'Although the main structure of the house is wood, it contains neither nails nor screws but is pinned together with wooden pegs. The main beams appear to be pre-Norman and still in good condition'.

72. These old houses in Alma Street, Woodlesford, were probably built in the eighteenth century to house families working at the papermill. The chimney to the mill shows above the roof of the house at the end of the row; although in reality it is quite some distance away. The mill premises were later used by Mr. Oddie as a collection point for the output of local cottage lace makers. At the end of the last century Messrs. Seanor's of Rothwell Match Works made fireworks there. The gas for the street lamps and private homes was manufactured by Henry Bentley's Brewerey Company.

73. This railway was first known as the Leeds to Derby Railway. It was also the railway rejected by Rothwell. Its proper title was The North Midland Railway. At the date of this photo Messrs. Bentley's gas plant was situated on the west side of the road opposite the main entrance into the brewery (near the distant horse and cart). The rocks of the cutting on the corner of Station Lane once stood perpendicular above the road. They were scaled down after George Priestley, a passenger off the Leeds train, in thick fog, took the wrong way out of the station walked over the cliff end and was killed.

74. Premises at Swillington Bridge, end of Bullerthorpe Lane, outside of Rothwell parish, but well documented in the Rothwell Court Rolls. For some unknown reason farmers in this area, certainly in Colton not far away, were within the Soke of Rothwell, meaning they were obliged to bring their corn to Rothwell mill to be made into flour. A documentation of 655 A.D. says in that year the Mercian army of Penda attempted to cross the River Aire, at Woodlesford. In 1756 this farmhouse belonged John Clayton, skinner and copyholder of Rothwell Manor Court, who that year bought two cottages and land for £22.

75. Match this with the previous photograph for a fuller view of the area. It truly depicts the charm and quiet of pre-motoring days with tree lined roads and no traffic congestion. The gates are to Swillington Hall, the family home of the Lowthers, taken before they left and dereliction took over. Mr. Norman, gamekeeper to the estate, lived in the farm across the way at the beginning of this century. Sir William Lowther claimed to be Lord of the Manor of Rothwell and Hereditary Court Baron of Rothwell Manor Court Leet.

76. *Everything, no matter what, is a beginning and an ending:* and this book ends where it began with the star exhibit of the 1897 Jubilee. It shows the Committee formed to promote the Bullock Roasting. The beast cost £16. Its homeward journey was broken at the Unicorn, Carlton, to await the Committee to head it, and the Old Band, to play it into Rothwell. It was paraded through the streets with stops at all the public houses along the way. It took thirty-six hours to roast in a field between Whitehall farm and the Black Bull Hotel. On the day it was cut up and made into sandwiches to be sold at 3d. a time.